MANCHESTER
UNITED

by Todd Karpovich

SportsZone

EUROPE'S BEST
SOCCER CLUBS

abdopublishing.com

Published by Abdo Publishing, a division of ABDO, PO Box 398166, Minneapolis, Minnesota 55439. Copyright © 2018 by Abdo Consulting Group, Inc. International copyrights reserved in all countries. No part of this book may be reproduced in any form without written permission from the publisher. SportsZone™ is a trademark and logo of Abdo Publishing.

Printed in the United States of America, North Mankato, Minnesota
042017
092017

Cover Photos: Magi Haroun/Rex Features/AP Images, foreground; AP Images, background
Interior Photos: Ian Hodgson/Reuters/Newscom, 4, 36; Popperfoto/Getty Images, 7, 15; Adam Butler/ AP Images, 8, 12; Owen Humphries/Press Association/URN:12001859/AP Images, 11; Andreu Dalmau/ European Press Agency/Newscom, 16, 17; Bob Thomas/Popperfoto/Getty Images, 18; Press Association/ URN:10044788/AP Images, 21; Klaus Heirler/picture-alliance/dpa/AP Images, 23; Mirrorpix/Newscom, 24, 27, 32; Dean Bertoncelj/Shutterstock Images, 28; Scott Heppell/AP Images, 30; David Klein/Sportimage/ Cal Sport Media/Newscom, 35; Simon Bellis/Cal Sport Media/AP Images, 38; Magi Haroun/Rex Features/ AP Images, 41; Matthew Impey/Rex Features/AP Images, 42

Editor: Patrick Donnelly
Series Designer: Craig Hinton
Content Consultant: Paul Logothetis, European soccer reporter

Publisher's Cataloging-in-Publication Data

Names: Karpovich, Todd, author.
Title: Manchester United / by Todd Karpovich.
Description: Minneapolis, MN : Abdo Publishing, 2018. | Series: Europe's best
    soccer clubs | Includes bibliographical references and index.
Identifiers: LCCN 2016963090 | ISBN 9781532111358 (lib. bdg.) |
    ISBN 9781680789201 (ebook)
Subjects: LCSH: Soccer--Europe--History--Juvenile literature. | Soccer teams--
    Europe--History--Juvenile literature. | Soccer--Europe--Records--Juvenile
    literature. | Manchester United (Soccer team)--Juvenile literature.
Classification: DDC 796.334--dc23
LC record available at http://lccn.loc.gov/2016963090

TABLE OF
CONTENTS

CHAPTER 1

THE TREBLE

Something special began in the early 1990s in Manchester, England. Talented young players began coming up through Manchester United's youth academy. There was versatile midfielder Paul Scholes. Then came defender Gary Neville. Others included midfielders Nicky Butt, Ryan Giggs, and David Beckham. Soon they were joined by midfielder Phil Neville, Gary's younger brother.

Each player moved on to the senior team. Each became a star in his own right. And they weren't the only ones. Sturdy Danish goalkeeper Peter Schmeichel had joined the team

EUROPEAN SOCCER

The European soccer season is broken down into different levels of competition. It can be confusing to keep track. Here's a handy guide to help you follow the action.

League Play

The 20 best teams in England play in the Premier League. Teams play all league opponents twice each season for 38 total games. The three teams with the worst records are relegated—or sent down—to the second division, which sends three teams up to replace them the next season. The Premier League debuted in 1992–93. It replaced the Football League First Division (1888–1991) as England's top league.

European Play

The top four teams in the Premier League qualify for the Union of European Football Associations (UEFA) Champions League. This annual tournament involves the best teams from the top leagues throughout Europe. The Champions League started in 1992. It replaced the European Cup, a similar tournament that began in 1955.

The next three teams in the Premier League qualify for the UEFA Europa League. The Europa League is Europe's second-tier tournament. It runs in a similar manner to the Champions League but crowns its own winner. The Europa League debuted in 1971 as the UEFA Cup but was renamed in 2009.

Domestic Cups

Almost every English team is eligible to play for the Football Association Challenge Cup (FA Cup). The tournament typically includes several hundred teams, including the professional teams from the Premier League. Founded in 1871–72, the FA Cup is the oldest soccer tournament in the world. The League Cup is a similar tournament. It involves teams from only the top four divisions in England.

Roy Keane became United's captain in 1997.

in 1991. Ireland's Roy Keane came in 1993. The team also added forwards Andy Cole of England and Dwight Yorke from Trinidad and Tobago. Both proved to be top goal-scoring threats.

Manchester United soon emerged as a top threat in the Premier League. By the fall of 1998, the team known as the "Red Devils" was ready to do something special. It all came together over a two-week stretch in May 1999.

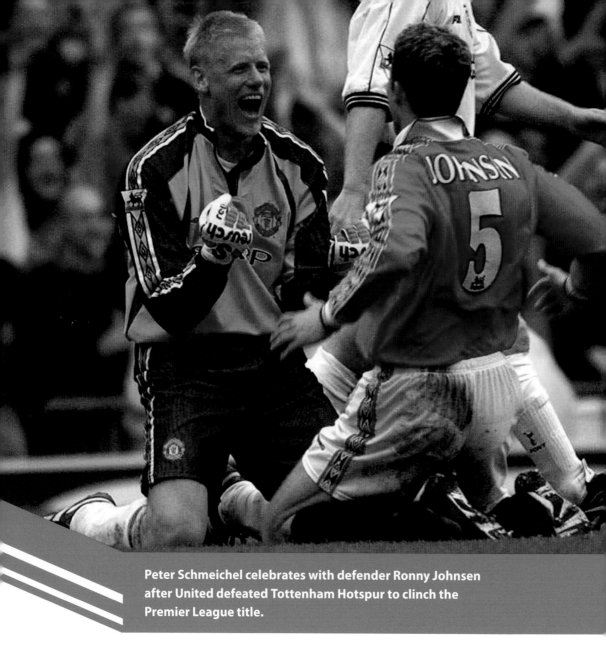

Peter Schmeichel celebrates with defender Ronny Johnsen after United defeated Tottenham Hotspur to clinch the Premier League title.

Racking Up Trophies

Top English soccer clubs play for two major trophies. One goes to the winner of the Premier League. The Red Devils and

Arsenal battled for first place throughout the season. It all came down to the final week. On May 16, Beckham and Cole scored as United posted a comeback win over Tottenham Hotspur. The victory gave United its third Premier League trophy in six seasons.

Next came the FA Cup. It's the oldest soccer tournament in the world. Almost every English team competes. United began in the third round in January. Over seven games, United marched its way to the final. This included a hard-fought two-game semifinal against Arsenal. Then a 2–0 victory over Newcastle United on May 22 gave the Red Devils their second major trophy of the season. Winning two major trophies in a season is called a double. But Manchester United was seeking something more historic: a treble. That's when a team wins three trophies in the same season.

FAST FACT

The young players who came up through Manchester United's youth system were nicknamed "Fergie's Fledglings." The nickname referred to longtime manager Sir Alex Ferguson. Ryan Giggs, Gary Neville, and Paul Scholes each played their entire careers for United.

The Best of Europe

The greatest challenge was saved for last. Each year Europe's top club teams meet in a tournament. It's called the Champions League. Winning this title would give United the three biggest trophies it could win. No English team had ever achieved this feat.

Manchester United had won the tournament in 1968. Back then it was called the European Cup. However, no English team had been champions of Europe since Liverpool in 1984. United was out to break that streak.

FAST FACT

Peter Schmeichel was named captain for the Champions League final and came up with one of the best games of his storied career. It was his last game with the Red Devils.

Manchester United had survived 12 Champions League games over 10 months. On May 26, less than a week after its FA Cup triumph, United faced German power Bayern Munich for the title.

The game was played at the famous Camp Nou stadium in Barcelona, Spain. Fans from across Europe came to watch. United and Bayern Munich were among the world's most

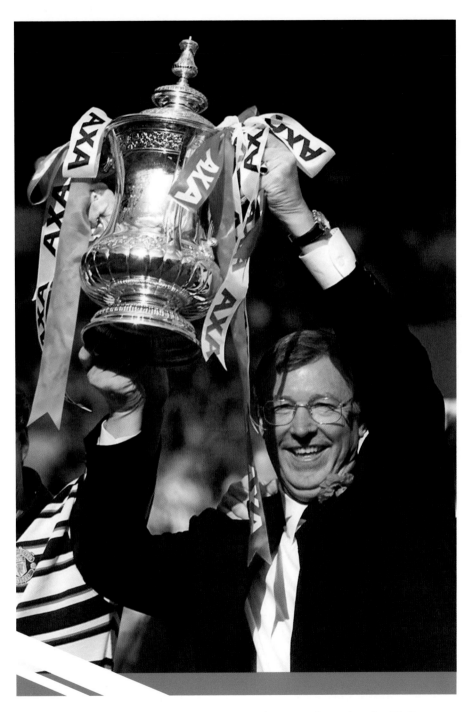

Sir Alex Ferguson hoists Manchester United's second trophy, the FA Cup, after a 2–0 defeat of Newcastle United.

popular teams. They took different approaches to the game. Manchester United was a crafty team that liked to attack. Bayern Munich focused on tight organization and precise passes to break down opponents. But the Germans had one key advantage. United midfielders Scholes and Keane were out due to suspension.

The Germans took advantage early. Munich was awarded a free kick on United's side of the field just six minutes into the game. The Manchester players formed a wall. But Bayern winger Mario Basler curled his shot around them. Schmeichel didn't see the ball until it was skipping past him. United was down 1–0.

United regrouped. The midfield of Giggs, Butt, Beckham, and Jesper Blomqvist began to control possession. But each time they attacked, Bayern's defense held strong. Unshakable goalie Oliver Kahn blocked every shot. On the other side of the field, Schmeichel stood strong for United. He stopped everything that came his way.

Bayern defender Michael Tarnat, left, thwarts a scoring chance by Manchester United's Ryan Giggs.

The second half proved to be more of the same. Neither team could beat the other's legendary goalie. Dreams of a Manchester United treble began to fade as the clock neared 90 minutes. Finally, the referees indicated three minutes of stoppage time. It was now or never for United.

Last-Minute Heroics

The Champions League winner's trophy was brought to the sidelines. The Bayern Munich reserves began to celebrate on the bench. It was a bit premature. United was awarded a corner kick. Beckham lined up and swerved the ball to the top of the penalty area. Giggs was waiting for it. He sent it toward the goal, and second-half substitute Teddy Sheringham redirected the ball past Kahn. One minute into stoppage time the game was tied 1–1.

Bayern Munich's fans looked on in disbelief. Its players were shocked. Manchester players and supporters celebrated. The momentum had now swung completely in United's favor. But the drama wasn't over just yet.

Only moments remained in regulation. Then Beckham once again made a key cross to the penalty area. This time, Sheringham leaped above a defender and headed the ball.

Teddy Sheringham outleaps the Bayern Munich defense and heads the ball toward the net to set up United's second goal.

Dejected Bayern Munich players react to their shocking loss to Manchester United in the 1999 Champions League final.

Teammate Ole Gunnar Solskjaer slipped behind the defense. He rocketed the ball into the top of the net for a goal. With all hope seemingly lost just minutes earlier, United now led 2–1.

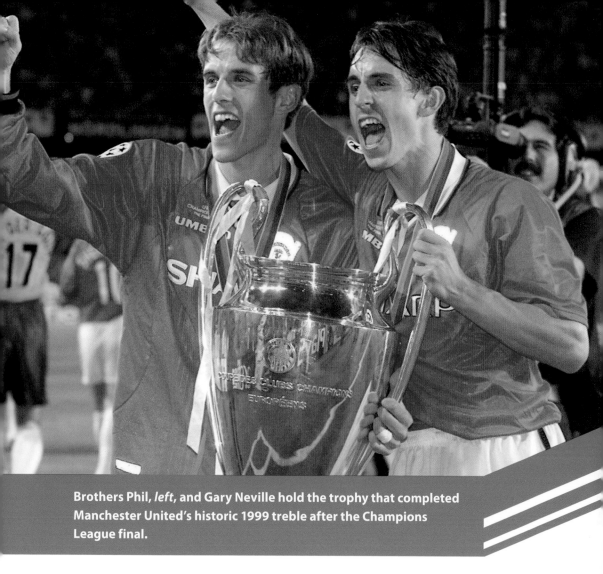

Brothers Phil, *left*, and Gary Neville hold the trophy that completed Manchester United's historic 1999 treble after the Champions League final.

The referee soon blew his whistle, and Manchester United had completed one of the greatest comebacks in Champions League history. Manchester United became the first English club to win the treble. United cemented its place as one of the greatest teams in the world.

CHAPTER 2

HUMBLE BEGINNINGS

The first official soccer rules were written in 1848. Manchester United was founded only 30 years later. The team began as the Newton Heath LYR Football Club (FC) in 1878. The first players were workers at the Lancashire and Yorkshire Railway depot. In 1902 the club changed its name to Manchester United. It soon began wearing its trademark red jerseys. Today Manchester United is one of the world's most popular teams.

The team began playing in England's First Division in 1892–93. Manchester United's first great successes came

15 years later. Coach Ernest Mangnall led the club to league titles in 1908 and 1911. Manchester United also took home its first FA Cup championship in 1909.

United hit a long drought after its second league title. Two world wars ravaged Europe. Manchester United's stadium, known as Old Trafford, was almost completely destroyed by German bombers during World War II (1939–1945).

Busby Era

United's fortunes changed when Sir Matt Busby took over as manager in 1945. His arrival was a key factor in turning Manchester United into one of England's top clubs. Busby was a former player for rivals Manchester City and Liverpool. His first priority was to restore Old Trafford. He then shifted his focus to signing England's top players. He put together one of Europe's stingiest defenses with Johnny Carey, John Aston, and Allenby Chilton. For the attack, Busby signed creative players such as Charlie Mitten,

FAST FACT

Manchester United's Allenby Chilton was the backbone of one of the stingiest defenses in all of Europe. He was also a national hero. He fought on the beaches of Normandy during World War II.

Sir Matt Busby, *right*, sizes up fellow Scotsman Denis Law.

Jack Rowley and Stan Pearson. It didn't take Busby long to build a winner. Manchester United won its second FA Cup with a 4–2 victory over Blackpool in 1948.

The success did not stop there. Manchester United pushed for league championships from 1947 through 1949. But United finished second each time. The club made another run in 1951. But once again it was a runner-up. United finally brought home a championship in 1952. It was the club's first league title in 41 years. United clinched at Old Trafford with a 6–1 victory over Arsenal.

Busby was able to develop a scouting department that kept its eyes on the top young players around England. He convinced many to play for United. Players such as Bill Foulkes, Mark Jones, David Pegg, and Liam Whelan eventually cracked the starting lineup. This generation of players became known as "Busby Babes." United won league titles in 1956 and 1957. The club also reached another FA Cup final in 1957. United had all of the building blocks for success. But tragedy changed its fortunes again.

A Dark Day

February 6, 1958, was the saddest day in the history of Manchester United. The team was returning from a European Cup game against Red Star Belgrade in the former Yugoslavia.

Snow falls on the wreckage of the plane that crashed in Munich, West Germany, in 1958, killing eight United players.

The plane crashed shortly after taking off from an airfield in Munich, West Germany.

Busby was part of the 44-person traveling party. He was hospitalized in critical condition for weeks. But he survived his injuries. However, eight United players were among the

23 people who did not. Jones, Pegg, and Whelan were killed. So were five other players and three staff members.

When Busby recovered, he was determined to honor the fallen players. The depleted roster fell short of winning a third straight league championship. United also lost to Bolton in the FA Cup final. But Busby quickly restocked his team. Together they started a new era of Manchester United soccer.

A New Dawn

The turnaround had begun by the early 1960s. United took home its third FA Cup title in 1963 with a 3–1 victory over Leicester City. United then won league championships in 1965 and 1967. Busby laid the foundation that would keep United on track for years to come.

In 1968, the 10-year anniversary of the plane crash, United reached the final of the European Cup. It played against Benfica, a club from Portugal. The score was tied 1–1 after 90 minutes. Then United erupted for three goals in extra time for a 4–1 victory. Captain Bobby Charlton scored twice. United became the first English club

Bobby Charlton leads Manchester United onto the field in 1965.

to win the European Cup in its 13-year history. Three years later, Busby retired.

Fergie Restores Order

United hadn't finished higher than third place in England's First Division from 1980 until the end of the 1986 season. That didn't meet the championship standards established by Busby, who retired in 1971. It all changed on November 6, 1986. Manchester United gambled on a little-known Scotsman to manage the team. The brash Alex Ferguson wasted no time putting his stamp on English soccer.

Ferguson is regarded as the most successful manager in British soccer history. He won 13 Premier League titles, five FA Cups, and two Champions League titles in 27 years with United. And United became one of the most popular teams in the world during this time. In all, he took home 38 trophies with Manchester United before retiring in 2013.

FAST FACT

George Best made his Manchester United debut in 1963 at the age of 17. He scored his first goal in just his second game. He's remembered as one of the most talented forwards to ever play the game.

George Best surveys the field during a 1968 game.

CHAPTER 3

ONE OF A KIND

Few sports teams are more recognizable than Manchester United. The fans' adoration stretches beyond the record number of wins. The club has established a culture of producing players who are driven to live up to its motto: "Youth, Courage, Greatness." Old Trafford draws visitors from around the globe and not just United supporters. The stadium is a must-see for any avid soccer fan.

Manchester United has produced some of the world's best players. Bobby Charlton, George Best, and David Beckham

Old Trafford has become a mecca of sorts for soccer fans around the globe.

became household names as they led United to incredible success on the field.

United enters each game with a target on its back. Clubs want to reward their loyal followers with a good showing against the mighty Red Devils. Due to United's success, the team has played in many important games. As such, many teams consider Manchester United to be their rival.

For United fans, however, there is no greater nemesis than Liverpool. The cities sit just 35 miles (56 km) apart. The clubs' first meeting was in 1894. They became the two most successful English clubs ever.

United's other main rival plays just 4 miles (6 km) away from Old Trafford. Geography makes Manchester City a natural foe. However, for many years the "Manchester Derby" wasn't very competitive. That changed when Manchester City got new ownership in 2008. Now when the teams meet, league titles—not just city bragging rights—are often on the line.

United is also one of the most profitable sports teams in the world. A 2016 survey ranked United fifth in the world with a value of $3.3 billion. Only the Dallas Cowboys, Real Madrid, FC Barcelona, and the New York Yankees are worth more.

FAST FACT

Manchester United holds the record for the largest margin of victory in a Premier League game. The Red Devils beat Ipswich Town 9–0 in 1995.

CHAPTER 4

STARS OF THE PAST

The plane crash in Munich left its mark on Manchester United. But the club recovered, and its resurgence was led by three top players. They would become known as the "Holy Trinity." Bobby Charlton was an English midfielder who survived the plane crash. George Best was a talented dribbler and goal scorer from Northern Ireland. Denis Law was a gifted Scottish forward who went on to have a long career. These three players became the core of one of the golden eras in the long and storied history of Manchester United. They excelled under the guidance of Sir Matt Busby.

A Nucleus Forms

Sir Alex Ferguson oversaw the next phase of stars to play for United. Some of their top players were among the biggest names in English soccer.

Midfielder David Beckham became one of the world's most famous athletes. He was a brilliant passer. He could set up teammates with accurate crosses and corner kicks. But he might have been most dangerous on free kicks. Beckham could "bend" the soccer ball, making it swerve in the air to get past defenders.

He won six Premier League titles with United from 1992 to 2003. Beckham also starred for England's national team. He is the only English player to score a goal at three World Cups (1998, 2002 and 2006).

FAST FACT

In 1999 David Beckham married pop star Victoria Adams. She was a member of the popular British music group Spice Girls. She performed using the name "Posh Spice." The couple has four children.

Ryan Giggs played his entire 24-year professional career with Manchester United. He was a main cog in the midfield.

From left, Paul Scholes, Rio Ferdinand, and Ryan Giggs were longtime mainstays for the Red Devils.

Giggs retired in 2014 as the Premier League's all-time leader in assists with 162.

Paul Scholes was one of United's top playmakers. The midfielder played 18 seasons in Manchester. He scored 155 goals before retiring in 2013. One of Scholes' brightest moments was scoring the game-winning goal in the 2008 Champions League semifinal against Barcelona. United went on to win the title that year.

Gary Neville played with United from 1992 to 2011. Ferguson named him captain in 2005. He stayed in that role for five years.

Cristiano Ronaldo made himself a household name during his time with Manchester United.

Neville also made 85 appearances for England's national team. He was known for being a gritty and determined defender. Nicky Butt was an integral part of United's championship teams from 1992 to 2004. The crafty and durable midfielder played in 387 games for the Red Devils.

In more recent years, Rio Ferdinand starred for United for 12 seasons. The center back came over from West Ham United for a record transfer fee in 2002. Ferdinand won six Premier League titles in Manchester.

Cristiano Ronaldo was Ferdinand's teammate from 2003 to 2009. The dynamic forward from Portugal was just 18 when he signed with United. Ronaldo was on a team that gave United its first league championship in five years. He also was part of its 2008 Champions League title. Ronaldo was voted the best player in Europe in 2008 after scoring 30 goals. He won multiple titles and trophies with United. He also set another record with a $128 million transfer fee when he left for Real Madrid.

FAST FACT

Jersey No. 10 is revered in the soccer world. But United has a different tradition. Some of its best players have worn No. 7. They include David Beckham, Cristiano Ronaldo, and George Best. Bryan Robson and Eric Cantona also have worn the number.

CHAPTER 5

MODERN STARS

A golden generation of players had led Manchester United to the 1999 treble. By 2004, however, many of those players were either gone or getting older. The team needed a young star to lead the next generation. It found that star in teenager Wayne Rooney.

Rooney debuted with Everton in 2002 as a 16-year-old. By the time he joined United, he was considered one of the brightest young stars in England. The teenage striker led United with 11 Premier League goals in his first season. Afterward he was named England's Young Player of the Year. And he was only getting started.

Over the next several seasons, Rooney became one of the biggest stars for Manchester United and England's national team. In 2009–10 he led United with 26 goals and was named England's Player of the Year. Two years later he scored 27. Though not particularly tall at 5 feet 7 inches, Rooney was like a bulldog on the ball and had a knack for finding the back of the net.

Through 2017 Rooney had helped United win five Premier League titles and the 2008 Champions League. The team also won the 2016 FA Cup and the League Cup three times.

Moving Forward

By 2016 Rooney and Manchester United needed help. Sir Alex Ferguson resigned as manager after winning the 2012–13 Premier League title. The team changed managers twice over the next three seasons. It also missed the Champions League in two of them. Longtime Everton manager David Moyes replaced Ferguson. But he lasted less than a year. His replacement was Louis van Gaal, who had managed such major European powers as Barcelona and Bayern Munich. He also led the Netherlands

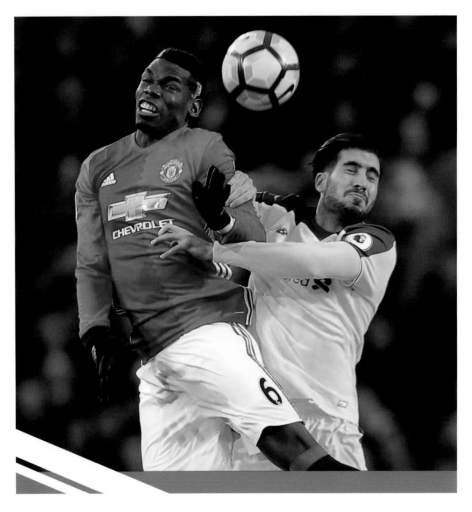

Paul Pogba, *left*, battles a Liverpool defender in 2017.

to the 2014 World Cup semifinals. But he couldn't match that success with United.

So another new manager was brought in to turn things around in 2016. José Mourinho had won championships at numerous clubs around Europe. He led Porto, Chelsea, Inter Milan, and Real Madrid to titles. But along the way he battled

David De Gea makes an acrobatic save against Watford in 2016.

owners, referees, and opposing coaches. This made him a controversial figure. But his success is undeniable.

Mourinho was hired to restore greatness at Old Trafford. He quickly assembled a lineup of star players. United signed striker Zlatan Ibrahimović. The native of Sweden has played for title-winning clubs throughout Europe. His imposing size is a challenge for even the most hard-nosed defenders. Ibrahimović scored the deciding goal in his United debut, immediately winning over the fans of the city of Manchester.

Paul Pogba earned world-class status while playing for Juventus in Italy. The tall, lanky forward can score from distance or jump over defenders to head the ball into the net. Pogba was just 23 years old when he joined United in 2016.

Scorers typically get most of the attention. But goalkeeper David De Gea made a huge impact. The Spanish star joined United in 2011. He became the first player to win the club's player of the year award three years in a row. De Gea consistently comes up with big saves to keep his team in the game. He is also a natural leader who keeps the defense organized. When United's defense has a rare breakdown, De Gea is often there to save the day.

FAST FACT

José Mourinho has not only won championships in four countries. He also won Champions League titles with Inter Milan and Porto.

MANCHESTER UNITED
TEAM FILE

NAME: Manchester United

YEAR FORMED: 1878 as Newton Heath LYR Football Club; changed name to Manchester United in 1902

WHERE THEY PLAY: Old Trafford, Manchester, England

FOOTBALL LEAGUE/PREMIER LEAGUE TITLES: 20
(most recent in 2012–13)

FA CUP TITLES: 12
(most recent in 2015–16)

LEAGUE CUP TITLES: 4
(most recent in 2009–10)

EUROPEAN CUP/CHAMPIONS LEAGUE TITLES: 3
(1967–68, 1998–99, 2007–08)

AUTHOR'S DREAM TEAM

GOALKEEPER: Peter Schmeichel

DEFENSE: Denis Irwin, Rio Ferdinand, Jaap Stam, Roger Byrne

MIDFIELD: Ryan Giggs, Bryan Robson, Bobby Charlton

FORWARDS: Cristiano Ronaldo, Denis Law, George Best

KEY RECORDS

- Largest margin of victory (top flight level): 9–0 vs. Ipswich Town, 1995

- Longest league winning streak: 11 games, March 11–May 14, 2000

- Most wins in a season: 28 (seven times, the most recent 2012–13)

- Most league goals in a season: 97, 1999–2000

TIMELINE

1878

Newton Heath LYR Football Club is founded.

1902

The club formally changes its name to Manchester United.

1908

Manchester United wins its first English league title.

1910

The club begins playing its home games at Old Trafford.

1945

The legendary Sir Matt Busby takes over as manager.

1958

The team plane crashes in Germany, killing 23 people, including eight players.

1968

The club wins its first European Cup.

1986

Alex Ferguson is named manager.

1993

Manchester United wins its first English league title since 1967.

1999

The club takes the treble: titles in the Premier League, FA Cup, and Champions League.

2013

Ferguson retires having won 13 Premier League titles, five FA Cups, and two Champions League titles.

2016

José Mourinho is named manager.

GLOSSARY

academy

A system for professional clubs that helps develop young players.

crafty

Clever at achieving one's aims.

debut

First appearance.

derby

An ongoing competition between two teams from the same region or city.

forward

A player positioned closest to the opponents' goal, ahead of most of his or her teammates.

generation

A group of people who are similar in age and other identifying characteristics.

integral

Important, vital.

penalty area

The box in front of the goal where a penalty kick is awarded if a player is fouled.

rivals

Opponents with whom a player or team has a fierce and ongoing competition.

scouting

Looking for talented players to join your team.

stoppage time

Time the referee can add to the end of a game to make up for time lost to injuries and other stoppages; also known as injury time.

transfer fee

The amount of money paid by one club to another for the right to sign one of its players to a contract.

FOR MORE INFORMATION

BOOKS

Kortemeier, Todd. *Total Soccer*. Minneapolis, MN: Abdo Publishing, 2017.

Marthaler, Jon. *Soccer Trivia*. Minneapolis, MN: Abdo Publishing, 2016.

McDougall, Chrös. *The Best Soccer Players of All Time*. Minneapolis, MN: Abdo Publishing, 2015.

WEBSITES

To learn more about Manchester United, visit abdobooklinks.com. These links are routinely monitored and updated to provide the most current information available.

PLACE TO VISIT

OLD TRAFFORD MUSEUM & TOUR CENTRE

Old Trafford (Sir Matt Busby Way)
Manchester M16 0RA
Phone: + 44 161 868 8000
www.manutd.com/en/Visit-Old-Trafford/Museum-And-Stadium-Tour/Museum.aspx

Take a firsthand look at one of the most venerable stadiums in the world. Also, get an even closer view of Manchester United and share 130 years of history in the stadium museum.

INDEX

ABOUT THE AUTHOR

Todd Karpovich is an award-winning writer based in Baltimore, Maryland. He has written for ESPN.com, the Associated Press, MLB.com, Sports Xchange, the *Baltimore Sun*, and other national media outlets. He is the coauthor of *Skipper Supreme: Buck Showalter and the Baltimore Orioles*.